The Map

by
Linda Kita-Bradley

Grass Roots Press

The Map is published by

Grass Roots Press, a division of Literacy Services of Canada Ltd.
Phone: 1-888-303-3213
Website: www.grassrootsbooks.net

ACKNOWLEDGMENTS

We acknowledge the financial support of the Government of Canada through the Canada Book Fund (CBF) for our publishing activities.

Produced with the assistance of the Government of Alberta, Alberta Multimedia Development Fund.

Government of Alberta ■

Editor: Dr. Pat Campbell
Photography: Grass Roots Press
Book design: Lara Minja, Lime Design Inc.

Library and Archives Canada Cataloguing in Publication

Kita-Bradley, Linda, 1958–
    The map / Linda Kita-Bradley.

ISBN 978–1–926583–77–8

    1. Readers for new literates. 2. Readers—Map reading.
3. Readers—Humor. I. Title.

PE1126.N43K5853 2012   428.6'2   C2011–907583–0

Printed in Canada

This is Sam.

Sam is new in town.

Sam has a map.

Sam wants to go to the bank.

Sam wants to go to the mall.

Sam walks down her street.

She turns left.

She turns right.

Where is the bank?

Sam looks at the map again.

She turns left.

She turns right.

Sam walks and walks.

Where is the mall?

■

Sam looks at the map again.

Sam walks.

She turns left.

What!

Sam is at home!

Sam looks at the map again.

Oh no!

The map is upside down!